AF228602

TESTING AND TREATMENT
THEN AND NOW

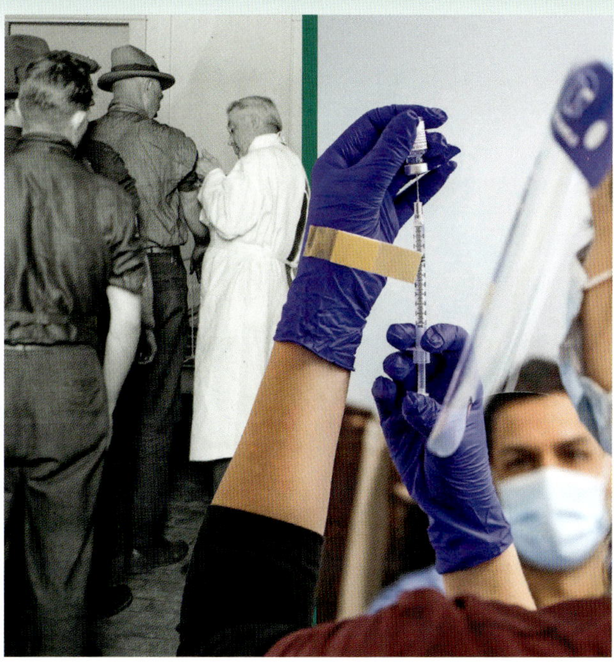

Abdo & Daughters
MIDDLE GRADE NONFICTION
An imprint of Abdo Publishing
abdobooks.com

Elsie Olson

ABDOBOOKS.COM

Published by Abdo Publishing, a division of ABDO, PO Box 398166, Minneapolis, Minnesota 55439. Copyright © 2022 by Abdo Consulting Group, Inc. International copyrights reserved in all countries. No part of this book may be reproduced in any form without written permission from the publisher. Abdo & Daughters™ is a trademark and logo of Abdo Publishing.

Printed in the United States of America, North Mankato, Minnesota

052021

092021

Design: Kelly Doudna, Mighty Media, Inc.

Production: Mighty Media, Inc.

Editor: Jessica Rusick

Cover Photographs: Erin Clark/AP/Shutterstock Images (right); National Archives and Records Administration

Interior Photographs: AP Images, pp. 7, 19, 23, 24–25; CDC Global/Flickr, pp. 16–17; CDC/Science Photo Library, p. 21; Erin Clark/AP/Shutterstock Images, p. 1 (right); Jae C. Hong/AP Images, pp. 26, 36–37; James Gathany/CDC, pp. 22, 33; MarylandGovPics/Flickr, p. 43; National Archives and Records Administration, pp. 1, 8–9, 10, 11, 13, 14–15, 44; The National Guard/Flickr, p. 34; NIAID/Flickr, p. 20; NIH/Flickr, p. 41; Patrick Semansky/AP Images, pp. 4–5; Shutterstock Images, pp. 6, 28, 29, 30–31, 32, 35, 45; Ted S. Warren/AP Images, pp. 27, 40; The White House/Flickr, p. 38

Design Elements: Shutterstock Images

LIBRARY OF CONGRESS CONTROL NUMBER: 2020949731

PUBLISHER'S CATALOGING-IN-PUBLICATION DATA

Names: Olson, Elsie, author.

Title: Testing and treatment: then and now / by Elsie Olson

Other title: then and now

Description: Minneapolis, Minnesota : Abdo Publishing, 2022 | Series: Pandemics | Includes online resources and index

Identifiers: ISBN 9781532195617 (lib. bdg.) | ISBN 9781098216344 (ebook)

Subjects: LCSH: Medical screening--Juvenile literature. | Medical examinations--Juvenile literature. | Medical supplies--Juvenile literature. | Epidemics--History--Juvenile literature. | Diseases and history--Juvenile literature. | Medical archaeology--Juvenile literature

Classification: DDC 614.5--dc23

TABLE OF CONTENTS

In October 2020, artist Suzanne Brennan Firstenberg planted roughly 240,000 white flags in Washington, DC. Each flag represented a US COVID-19 victim.

Chapter 1

WHEN VIRUSES ATTACK

There are more viruses on Earth than stars in the universe. Most are harmless. But some viruses cause infectious diseases in humans. Every year, viruses sicken billions of people around the world. Many of these infections are minor. But some viral diseases can be deadly.

In late 2019, a new coronavirus was discovered in China. Coronaviruses cause upper respiratory infections in humans. They are often responsible for common colds. But the new coronavirus was much deadlier and more contagious than a typical one. Scientists called the new virus SARS-CoV-2. The disease it caused was named COVID-19.

A Pandemic Begins

After its discovery, COVID-19 continued to spread quickly within China. By early March 2020, the disease had spread to hundreds of other countries. On March 11, the World Health

Organization (WHO) declared COVID-19 a pandemic. A pandemic occurs when a disease spreads throughout the world. During a pandemic, new infections occur in many different places at once.

It took the cooperation of leaders, public health officials, scientists, and medical workers around the world to fight the virus. Early in the pandemic, COVID-19 had no known treatment. So, medical workers had to figure out how best to save lives. The disease also shared many symptoms with influenza and common colds. Scientists had to develop tests to determine whether a sick person had COVID-19 or another illness. Scientists and pharmaceutical companies also got to work developing treatments and vaccines for the new viral threat.

COVID-19 was not the first pandemic to affect the world. In 1918, an influenza outbreak swept the globe. This pandemic was the deadliest in modern history. And due to the lack of scientific knowledge at the time, doctors and scientists were largely helpless to develop tests, treatments, and vaccines to fight it.

In 1918, influenza treatments largely included rest and hydration. Modern doctors have many other treatment options available. When someone is diagnosed with influenza, antiviral medications such as Tamiflu can help reduce the severity and length of the illness. In addition, influenza vaccines can help prevent people from getting influenza in the first place.

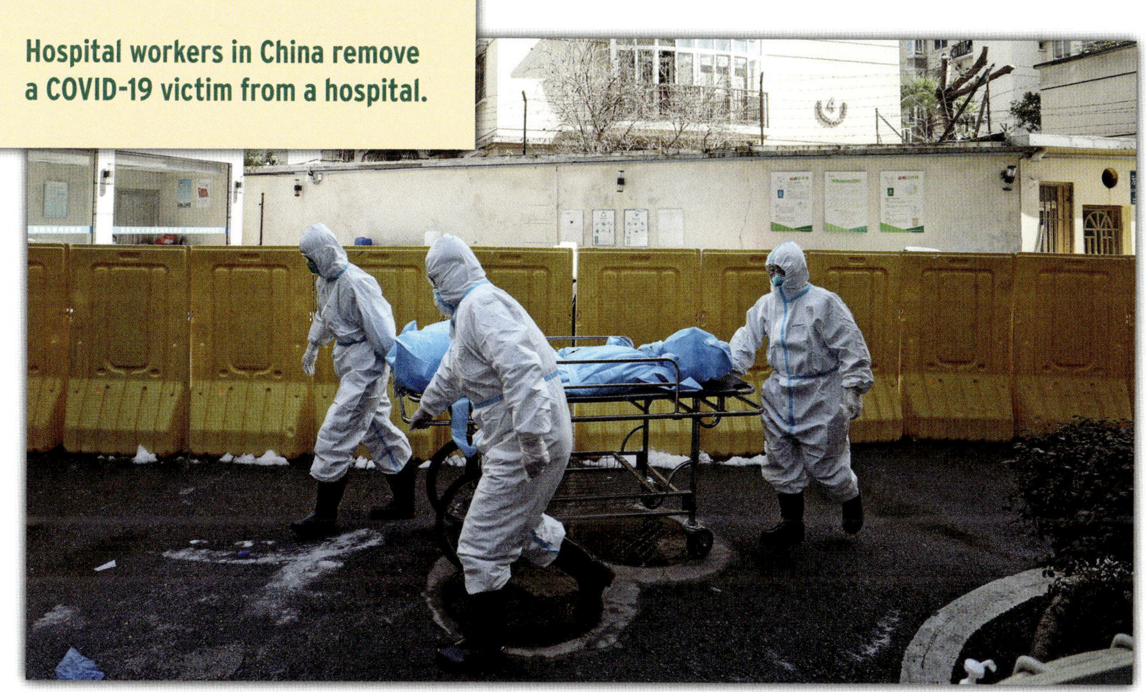

Hospital workers in China remove a COVID-19 victim from a hospital.

Soldiers in Texas line up to receive a preventative influenza throat spray. Despite claims, it did not prevent influenza.

Chapter 2

INFLUENZA IN 1918

In March 1918, influenza began affecting soldiers at Camp Funston, a US Army camp in Kansas. The illness sickened more than 1,000 of the camp's 54,000 soldiers, and 38 died. Modern scientists are still unsure where the virus originated. However, the outbreak at Camp Funston marked the first known cases of the pandemic.

Influenza, or the flu, is an upper respiratory infection. It commonly strikes in the United States in the fall and winter. This yearly period is known as flu season. Today, we know influenza is caused by a virus. But in 1918, viral science was a new area of study. Although scientists were familiar with the flu, they weren't certain what caused it. Some believed it was caused by germs called bacteria.

Outbreak and War

Influenza viruses have sickened humans for centuries. However, the 1918 influenza virus was unusual for several reasons. It was deadlier and more contagious than a typical flu virus. The disease also affected an unexpected population. Influenza is typically most deadly in people who are very old, very young, or who have health issues. But during the 1918 pandemic, many healthy young adults also became seriously ill.

War helped the influenza virus quickly spread around the world. In 1918, the United States and many other countries were fighting in World War I. That spring, the US military sent more than 100,000 troops abroad. The deadly virus traveled with them.

Influenza spreads through respiratory droplets released when people sneeze, cough, talk, or breathe. So, the disease spread

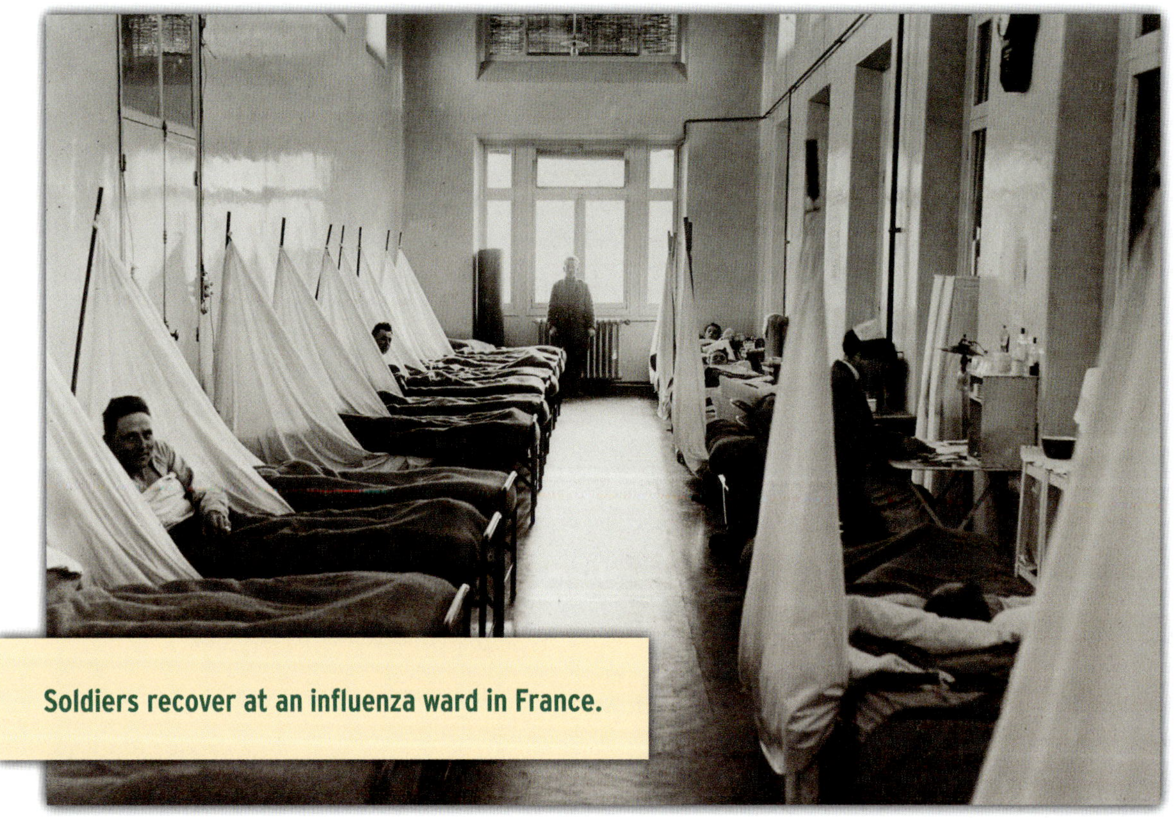

Soldiers recover at an influenza ward in France.

quickly within crowded military ships, trains, and living quarters. An estimated 45,000 US soldiers had died of the flu by the end of 1918. By the time the war ended in November 1918, the pandemic had spread to nearly every corner of the globe, sickening civilians and soldiers alike.

Three Waves

The 1918 pandemic struck in three waves. Infections peaked during each wave and dropped off between waves. The first wave began in the spring of 1918 and ended that summer. The second wave began in the fall of 1918. Viruses can mutate, or change, as they spread. During the second wave, a mutation made the virus more deadly and contagious. It was the deadliest wave of the pandemic.

The third and final wave began in January 1919. By summer, the pandemic was over. The virus had infected an estimated one-third of the world's population. Those who were infected had either died or become immune to the virus. Someone who is immune to a virus cannot be reinfected. So, over time, the virus infected fewer people and became extinct.

Tracking disease and death counts was not common at the time. So, no one knows exactly how many people died in each wave. But an estimated 50 million people around the world died during the pandemic, including 675,000 Americans.

PANDEMICS BY THE NUMBERS

ESTIMATED 1918 PANDEMIC CASES AND DEATHS

United States:
26 million cases
675,000 deaths

World:
500 million cases
50 million deaths

Treating the Flu

Doctors were unprepared to treat patients during the 1918 pandemic. There was no vaccine to prevent influenza. And, there were no antiviral drugs to make infections less severe. People ill with the virus were also more susceptible to bacterial infections such as pneumonia, which inflames the lungs. But antibiotics to treat bacterial infections would

Doctors attempted to develop influenza vaccines during the pandemic, but no vaccine was effective.

not be discovered for another decade. So, many influenza patients died from these secondary infections.

Most doctors gave influenza patients treatments typically used with other respiratory infections. These treatments included certain herbs, essential oils, and a medicine called quinine. Some doctors also believed whiskey helped stimulate patients' respiratory systems. This led to whiskey shortages across the United States. None of these treatments was proven to help treat influenza.

Other Techniques

Some doctors infused their sickest patients with blood from recovered influenza patients. Doctors had discovered this technique in the 1890s to treat some infections. Blood from a recovered patient temporarily provided a sick patient with virus-fighting proteins called antibodies. These proteins are produced by the body's immune system to fight infections. Studies later showed blood transfusion could reduce a patient's chance of dying by as much as 50 percent. However, blood transfusion was a relatively new practice. So, most doctors did not use the technique.

An outdoor influenza hospital in Lawrence, Massachusetts, treated hundreds of patients.

With no proven treatment, doctors relied largely on non-pharmaceutical measures to help patients. Doctors encouraged patients to rest and stay hydrated. Hospitals also focused on hygiene practices to keep germs from spreading. Medical workers frequently cleaned surfaces and washed their hands. They also did their best to keep patients isolated from one another. Germs can spread more easily in poorly ventilated areas. So, some hospitals set up open-air treatment centers. Here, patients were treated in outdoor tents. These centers had much lower death rates than many indoor hospitals.

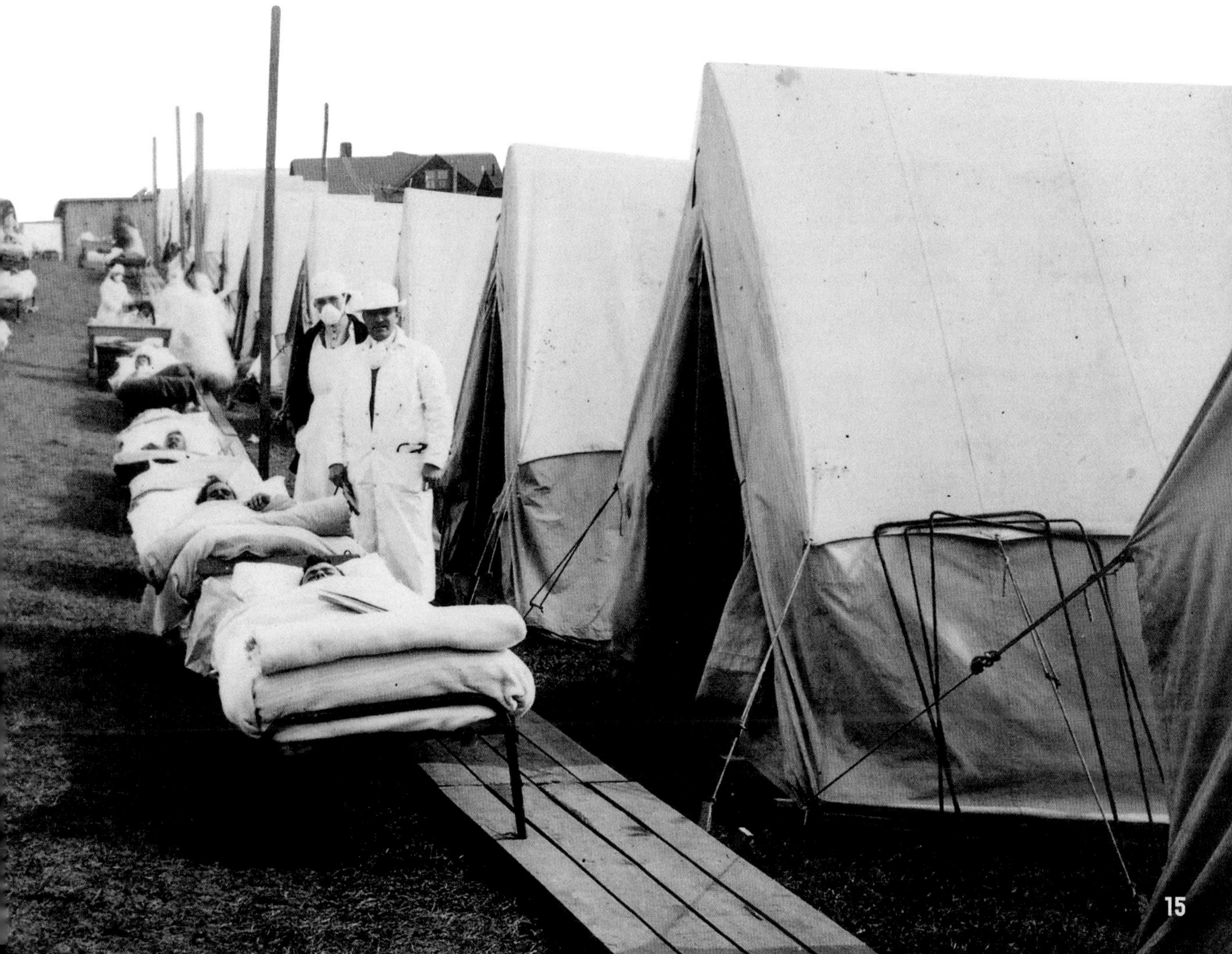

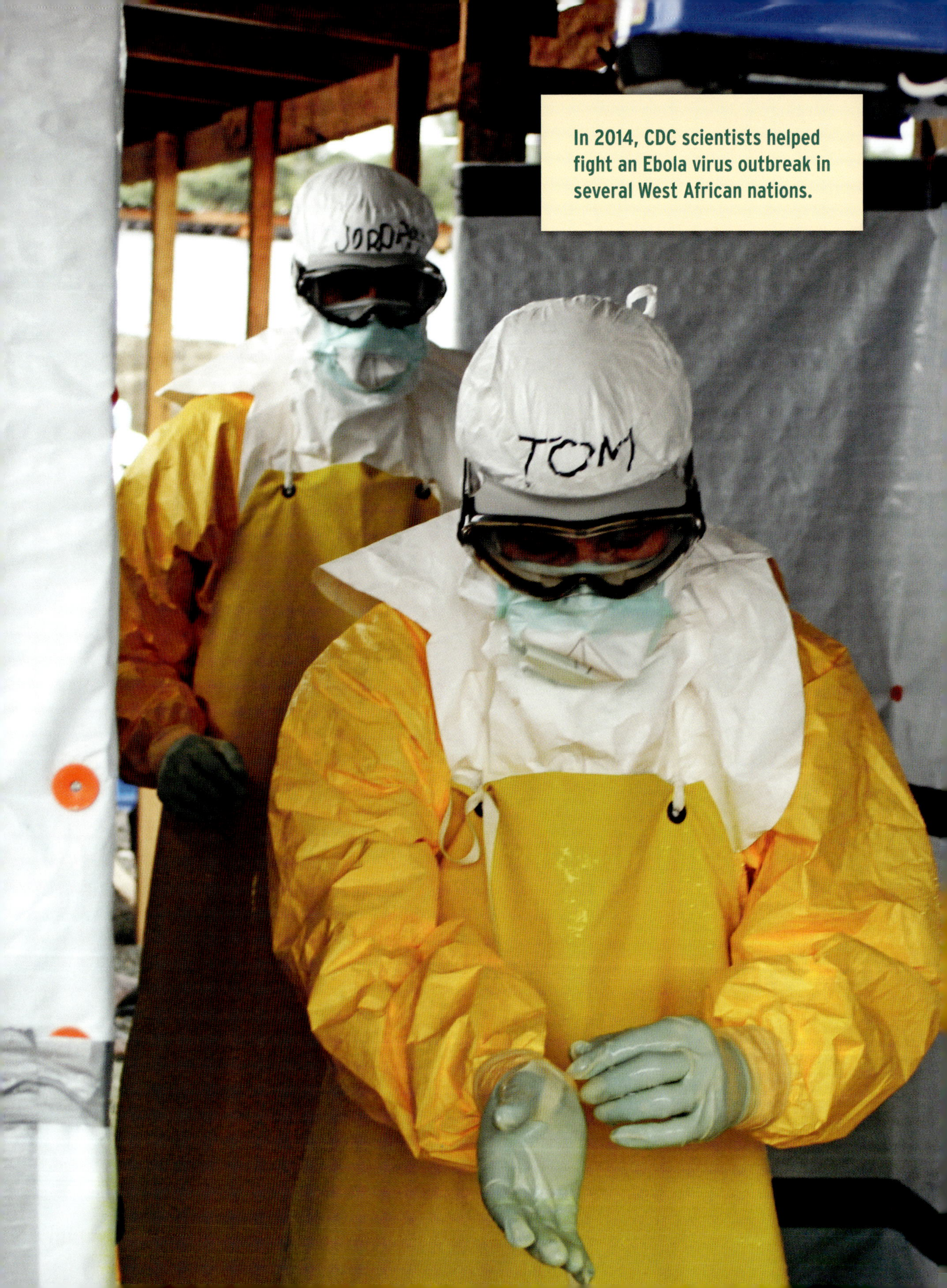

In 2014, CDC scientists helped fight an Ebola virus outbreak in several West African nations.

SCIENCE LEAPS FORWARD

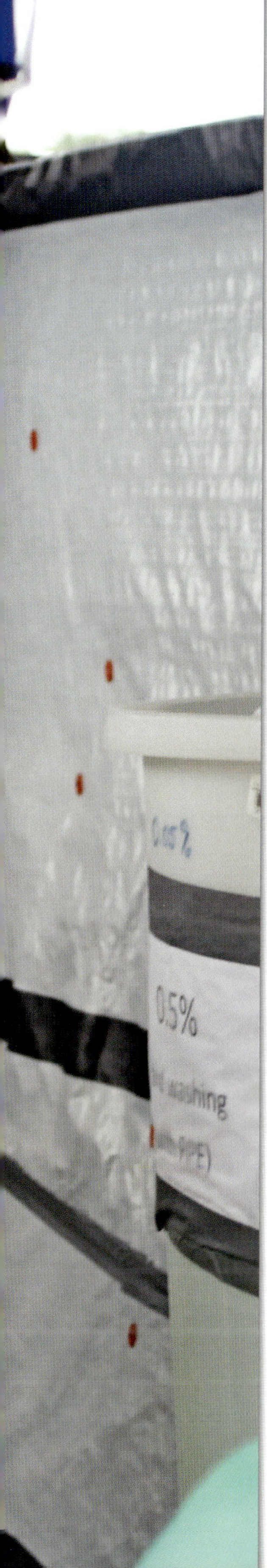

The 1918 pandemic killed more people than any other influenza pandemic before or since. Health officials in the United States and around the world were determined to learn from the crisis. That way, the world would be more prepared for future pandemics.

In 1918, public health policy had largely been determined by state and local governments. Over the next century, different federal and global health organizations formed to study, prevent, and inform the public about infectious diseases.

Organizing Health Care

In 1946, the Centers for Disease Control and Prevention (CDC) was founded in Atlanta, Georgia. The CDC soon became a leading voice on disease research and public health. Its scientists study how infectious diseases spread.

In 1948, the newly formed United Nations founded the WHO. The WHO's mission is to provide health services and medicines to people worldwide. It also advises governments on how to respond to health issues. And, it educates the public on healthy habits and disease prevention.

The US Department of Health, Education, and Welfare was founded in 1953. It was renamed the Department of Health and Human Services (HHS) in 1980. This cabinet department protects the health and well-being of Americans. It works closely with the CDC to set public health policy in the United States.

Digging Up a Virus

Scientists also worked to learn more about influenza viruses. In the early 1930s, researchers in London, England, isolated and observed the first influenza virus. This showed that the flu was caused by a virus and not bacteria.

As viral science developed, some researchers turned their attention back to the 1918 influenza virus. Scientists wanted to understand where it had originated and why it had been so deadly. In 1951, Swedish microbiologist Johan Hultin set out to solve the mystery. He traveled to Brevig Mission, a village in Alaska. The village had been hit hard by the 1918 pandemic. Seventy-two of the town's eighty adults had died from the flu. Their bodies were buried in a mass grave just outside of town.

Because of the frozen conditions, Hultin believed the bodies would be well preserved and still contain traces of the virus. Hultin

Hultin (*center*) shared his research with residents of Brevig Mission in 2005.

asked permission to take tissue samples from the bodies. He then tried to extract the virus from the samples. Hultin was unsuccessful at extracting the virus. But his work was not over.

Decoding the Virus

Decades later, Hultin got another chance to work with the 1918 virus. In 1997, he returned to Brevig Mission to collect another tissue sample. This time, he sent it to American pathologist Jeffery Taubenberger. Taubenberger had successfully isolated a portion of the 1918 virus's genetic material, using a different tissue sample a few years earlier. By examining the virus's genetic material, scientists could learn more about the virus's origins and makeup.

The sample Hultin sent to Taubenberger was better preserved than Taubenberger's original sample. In 1999, Taubenberger and other scientists used Hultin's sample to successfully study the 1918 virus's full genetic material.

Discoveries and Reconstruction

Influenza viruses come in four different types. These are A, B, C, and D. Each type has hundreds of different strains. Influenza A and B viruses cause seasonal influenza outbreaks. Of these two types, influenza A viruses often cause more serious infections. By studying the virus's genetic material, Taubenberger and his colleagues concluded that the 1918 flu virus was an influenza A virus. They also found that early versions of the virus had been spreading in humans since 1900.

In 2005, CDC scientists used the virus's genetic information to grow a live version of the virus. The scientists then infected laboratory mice with the virus to observe how deadly it was. The infected mice suffered severe lung infections. Most died in three days or less. The scientists

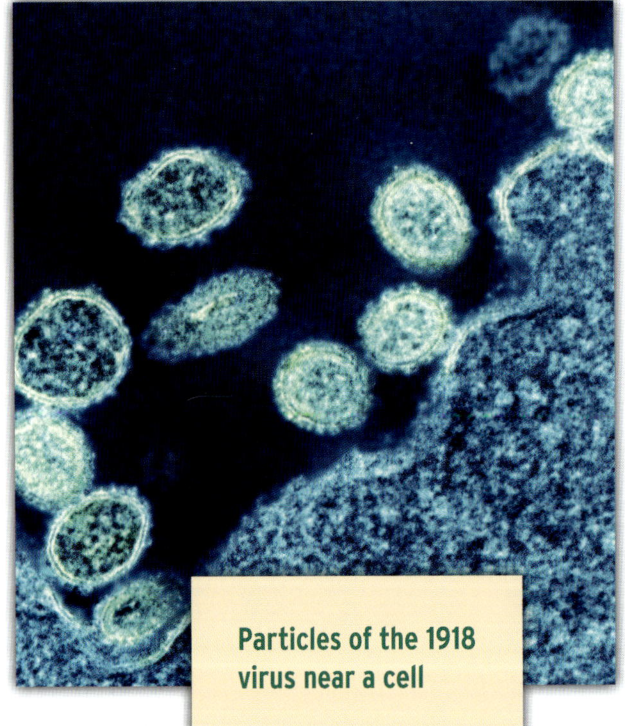

Particles of the 1918 virus near a cell

CDC scientists wore heavy protective equipment when studying the reconstructed 1918 virus.

also infected a group of mice with other flu viruses for comparison. Mice infected with the 1918 virus were 100 times more likely to die than mice infected with other flu viruses.

Vaccines

While some scientists worked to understand the 1918 virus, others worked to prevent future pandemics. In 1938, scientists developed the first influenza vaccine. Vaccines contain molecules called antigens that provoke an immune system response. In flu vaccines, the antigens are often inactive or weakened flu viruses. These viruses are not dangerous. However, they still cause the body's immune system to produce antibodies. These antibodies attack the

real virus if it enters
the body, preventing
infection.

The first flu vaccine
contained an inactive
influenza A virus.
It was tested on
members of the
US military. However,
studies showed
soldiers who received the vaccine were infected at similar rates
as those who had not been vaccinated. So, scientists continued
developing the vaccine.

In 1944, US soldiers received an improved flu vaccine. Civilians
received it the next year. Today, the CDC recommends that nearly
everyone aged six months and older receive a flu vaccine each
fall. Modern influenza vaccines are up to 60 percent effective at
reducing infections.

A flu vaccine can be administered via shot or nasal mist.

Antivirals

Vaccines could help prevent people from getting the flu. But they
did nothing to protect people who were already infected. In the
1960s, scientists began working to develop antiviral medications.
When a virus infects someone, it invades cells in the body and uses
them to replicate, or make copies of itself. These virus copies then
invade other cells. Antiviral drugs work by slowing this process.

In 1977, American scientist Gertrude Elion developed the first effective antiviral drug, acyclovir. It treated herpes viruses. These common viruses can cause cold sores and chicken pox. Other antivirals soon followed. In 1999, the US Food and Drug Administration (FDA) approved two new antiviral drugs, zanamivir and oseltamivir, to treat influenza. When taken soon after symptoms began, antivirals reduced the severity of symptoms and the length of the infection.

PIVOTAL PERSON: GERTRUDE ELION

For much of the 1900s, many scientists assumed viral infections were incurable. Scientist Gertrude Elion disagreed. In the 1940s, she developed a compound for a cancer drug. It showed antiviral properties. However, the compound was too toxic for use.

In the next decades, Elion developed drugs to treat nonviral diseases such as malaria. But in 1968, Elion reopened her research into antivirals. Over the next years, she and a team of scientists developed an antiviral compound called acyclovir to treat herpes viruses. In 1978, acyclovir was deemed safe to use. Elion won a Nobel Prize for her work in 1988.

Elion was inducted into the National Inventors Hall of Fame in 1991.

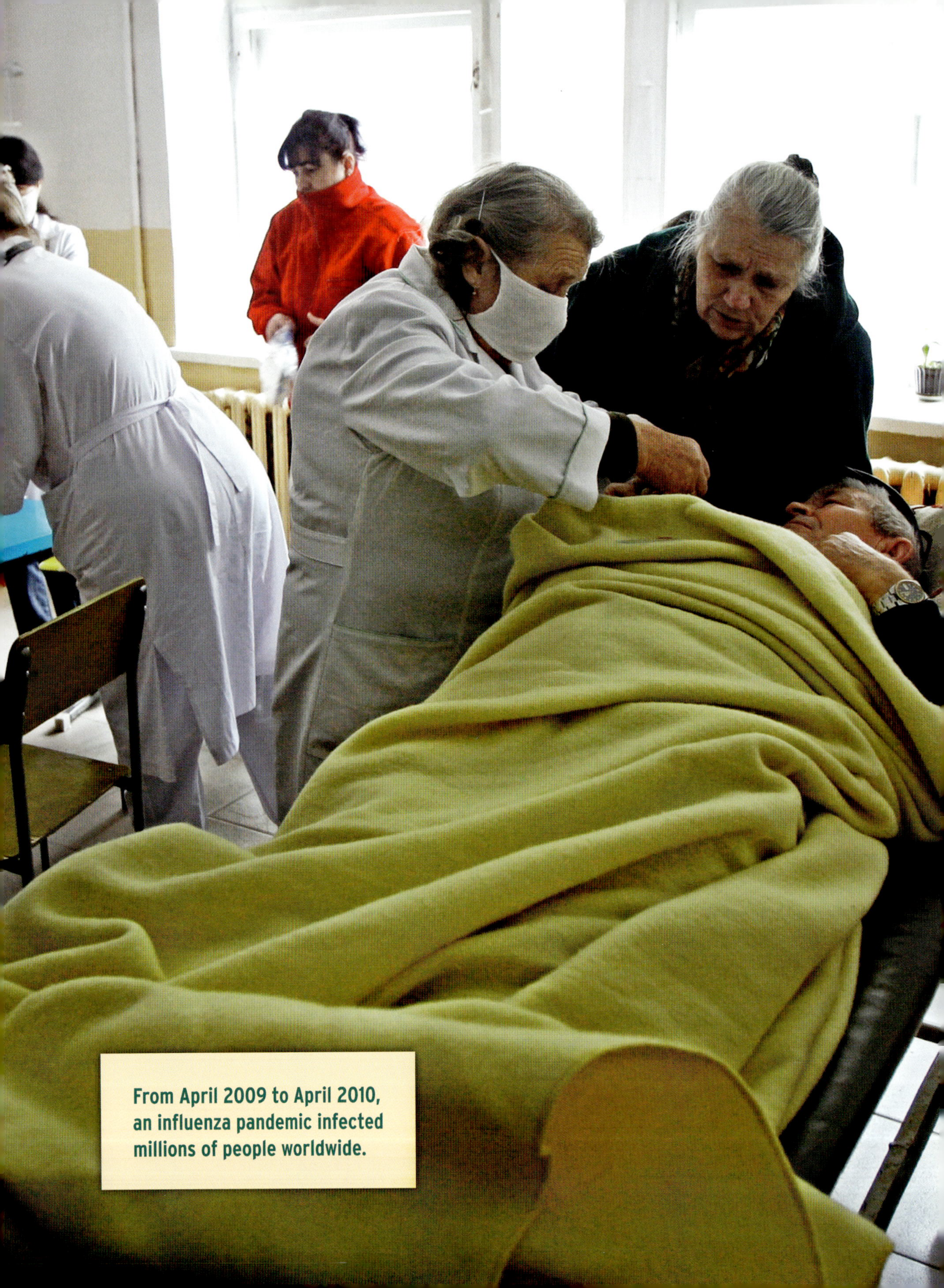

From April 2009 to April 2010,
an influenza pandemic infected
millions of people worldwide.

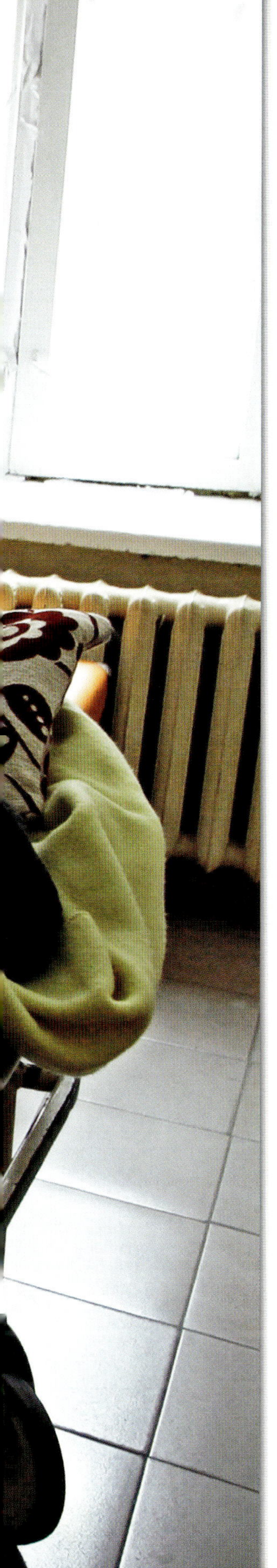

Chapter 4

A MYSTERIOUS VIRUS

Several viral pandemics struck the world between 1918 and 2020. None was as deadly as the 1918 flu pandemic. However, with viruses constantly spreading and mutating, public health experts warned that the next major pandemic was inevitable.

The first cases of the COVID-19 pandemic were identified in December 2019 in Wuhan, China. Hospitals across the city treated patients suffering from pneumonia of an unknown cause. Chinese scientists soon discovered the pneumonia was caused by a novel coronavirus, SARS-CoV-2. China reported the outbreak to the WHO on December 31.

A Viral Explosion

COVID-19 spread rapidly throughout Wuhan and other parts of China. Then, it spread worldwide. On January 13, 2020, the first

COVID-19 case was reported outside of China, in Thailand. The first US case was reported on January 20.

Most coronaviruses cause mild symptoms, including runny or stuffy nose, sneezing, and sore throat. But SARS-CoV-2 caused an unusually wide range of symptoms. These included fever, loss of taste or smell, headache, cough, shortness of breath, nausea, and diarrhea. Some people reported mild symptoms. Other people had no symptoms and could spread the virus without ever feeling sick.

Some people with COVID-19 became so sick they had to be hospitalized. The sickest COVID-19 patients experienced trouble

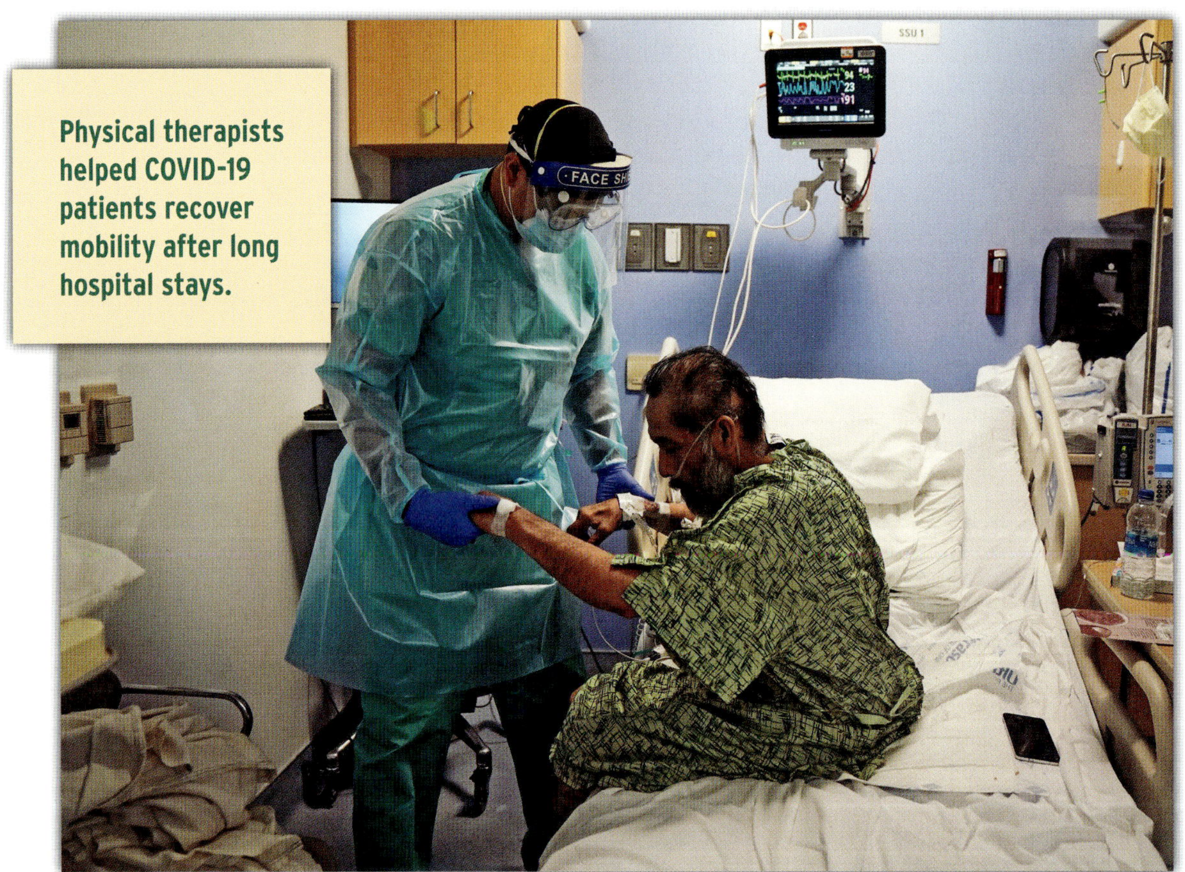

Physical therapists helped COVID-19 patients recover mobility after long hospital stays.

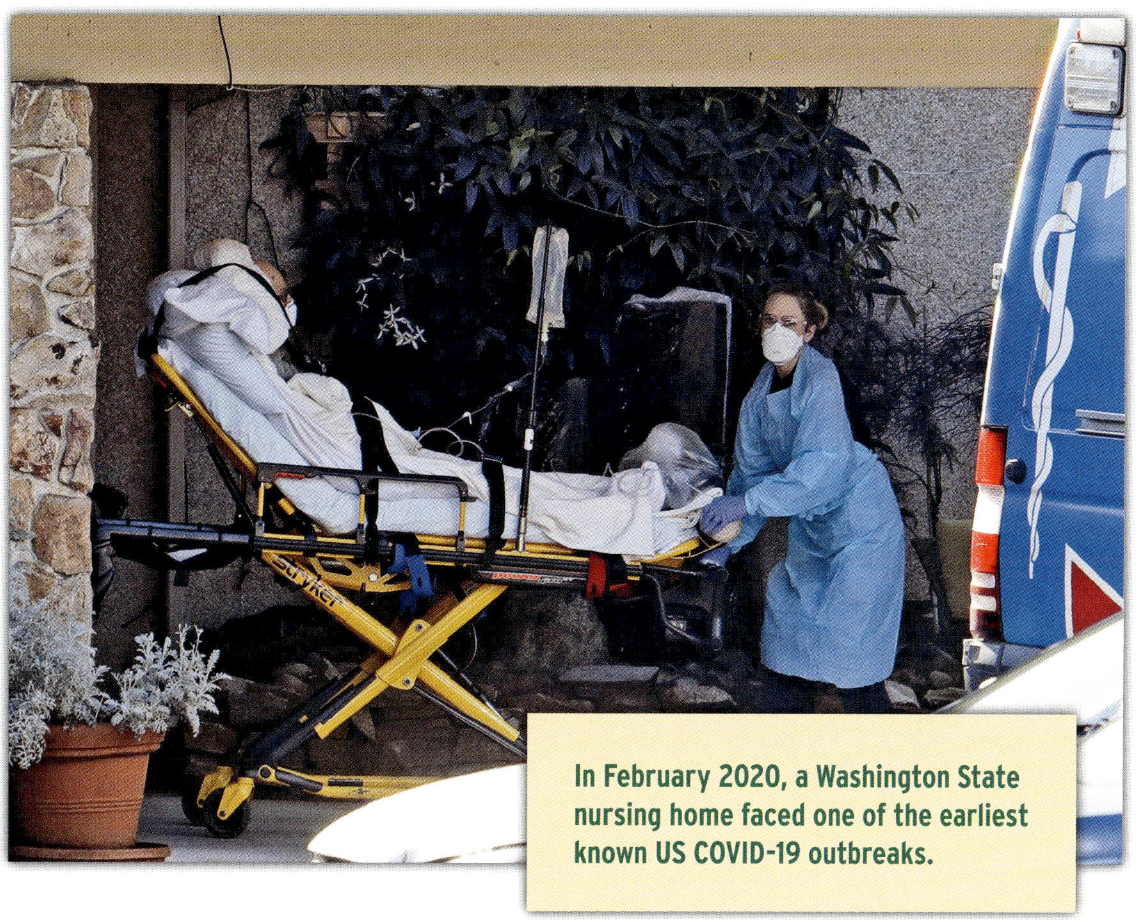

In February 2020, a Washington State nursing home faced one of the earliest known US COVID-19 outbreaks.

breathing and organ failure, which could lead to death. Elderly people or those with underlying health conditions, such as diabetes, were typically the most seriously affected. But some young and otherwise healthy people also became seriously ill.

COVID-19 symptoms could come on suddenly, turning from mild to serious in hours. Some people became seriously ill after initially appearing to recover. Most people who caught COVID-19 recovered in days or weeks. But others, known as long-haulers, experienced symptoms for months. Scientists and doctors struggled to understand why the virus affected people differently.

Early Treatments

Doctors scrambled to find effective treatments for COVID-19 patients. People with mild cases could often recover at home without visiting a hospital. Doctors recommended that these people rest, stay hydrated, and take pain relief medication to manage symptoms.

In severe cases, many hospitals used ventilators to help patients breathe. These machines pump air into and out of a person's airways. However, many hospitals had a limited number of these

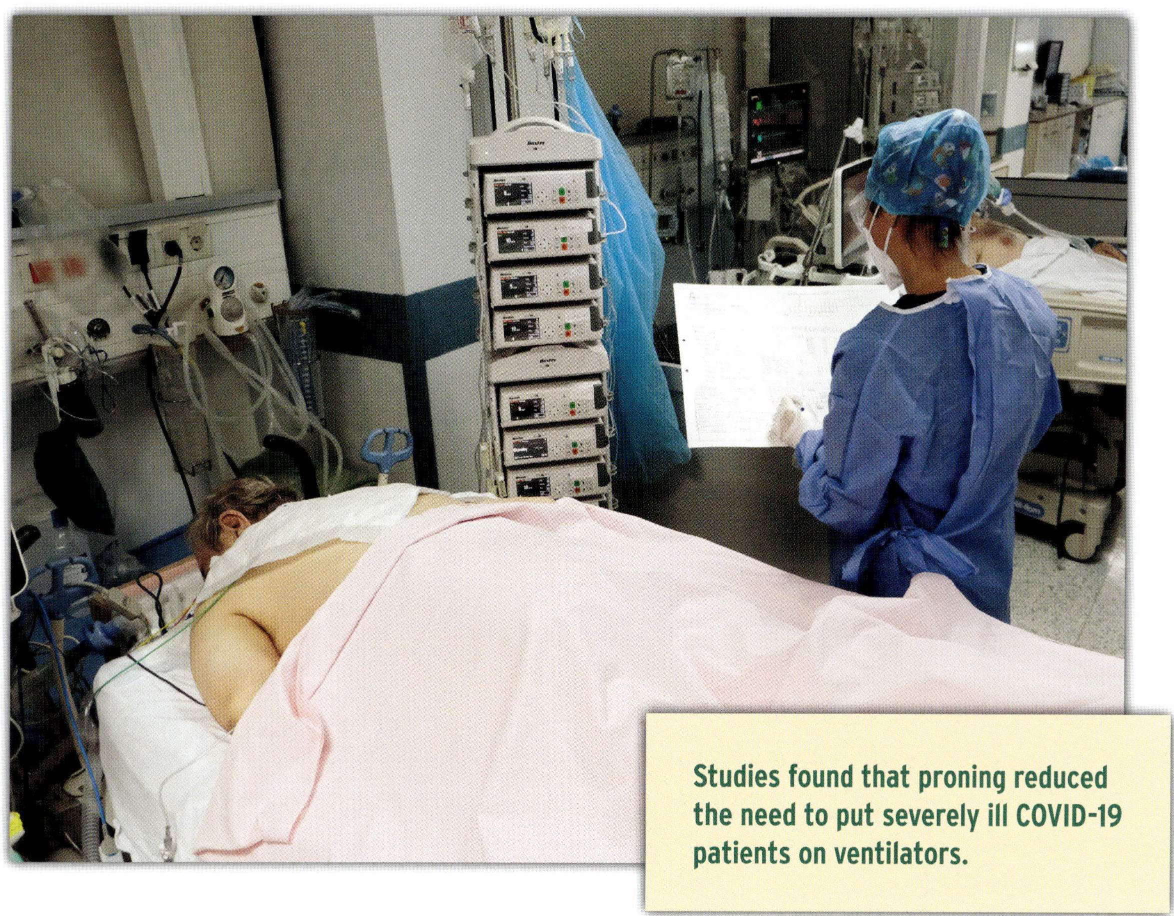

Studies found that proning reduced the need to put severely ill COVID-19 patients on ventilators.

machines. So, doctors often had to find other treatments. Some hospitalized patients received supplemental oxygen through oxygen masks. Medical workers also turned some patients onto their stomachs for part of each day. This practice, called proning, was found to make breathing easier for patients.

By summer 2020, medical workers had become experienced at caring for COVID-19 patients. So, hospitalized patients were more likely to recover than they had been early in the pandemic. But no treatment available could cure the disease. Instead, people simply had to take measures to slow COVID-19's spread.

People in Florida wear masks and socially distance as they wait in line at a post office.

Chapter 5

TESTING FOR COVID-19

Several measures helped slow COVID-19's spread. People wore face masks in public and avoided large gatherings. They also socially distanced from others by staying at least six feet (2 m) apart. COVID-19 testing was another way to slow the disease's spread. People who tested positive for the disease could quarantine, preventing others from being infected.

Soon after the virus was discovered, scientists worked to develop a test that could detect COVID-19. In early January 2020, Chinese scientists sequenced SARS-CoV-2's full genetic material. Researchers around the world used this information to develop COVID-19 tests for their countries. On January 17, 2020, the WHO published its first COVID-19 testing protocol, following a test developed by German researchers. Nations that had not developed their own tests could follow the protocol to make tests for their countries.

Testing Trouble

Different countries took different approaches to testing citizens. Some countries, including South Korea, tested many people quickly. By early February, South Korea encouraged all its citizens to get tested even if they weren't experiencing symptoms. Anyone who tested positive was told to quarantine. Anyone who had recently been in contact with an infected person was told to quarantine as well. Thanks to its aggressive early testing, South Korea had one of the lowest infection rates in the world in early 2021.

In the United States, the CDC developed its own COVID-19 test. The test kits were distributed to state laboratories

PANDEMICS BY THE NUMBERS

COVID-19 Rate by Country (January 2021)

UNITED STATES

Population: 330,062,181

Cases: 26,186,773

Cases per million people: 78,848

Deaths: 440,043

Deaths per million people: 1,325

SOUTH KOREA

Population: 51,296,082

Cases: 76,926

Cases per million people: 769

Deaths: 1,500

Deaths per million people: 27

By March 8, 2020, South Korea had administered more than 180,000 COVID-19 tests.

starting February 5. Unfortunately, many of the test kits didn't work properly. The CDC said the failure was likely due to contamination in its laboratory. It took another month for improved tests to be distributed around the country. In the meantime, COVID-19 spread throughout the United States.

During the testing shortage, the CDC only tested people who had recently traveled to China or who had a known virus exposure. That meant many people experiencing symptoms couldn't get tested. Some doctors and public health officials criticized the CDC and the federal government for failing to expand and improve COVID-19 testing. By the end of March, the CDC had fixed its test. In addition, the FDA had approved other tests developed by private laboratories. This allowed the United States to administer more than 100,000 tests a day. But it was too late to contain COVID-19's spread.

Test Types

The CDC developed two types of tests to diagnose COVID-19 infections. The first was administered by collecting a saliva sample or swabbing a person's nose or throat. Lab technicians then checked these fluids

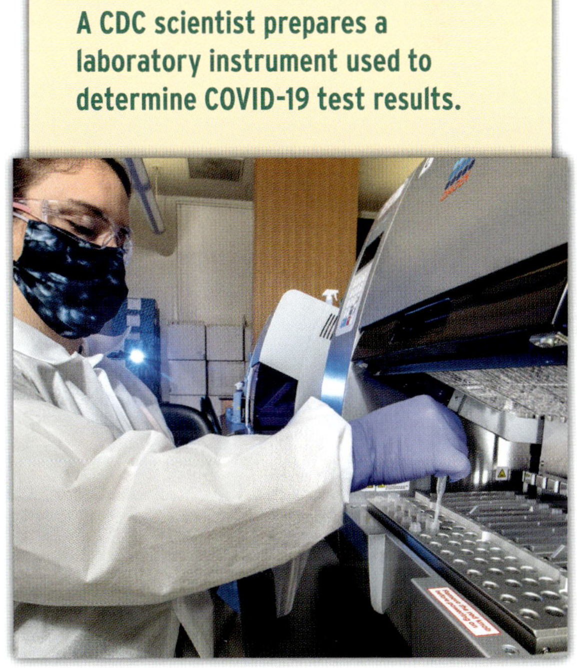

A CDC scientist prepares a laboratory instrument used to determine COVID-19 test results.

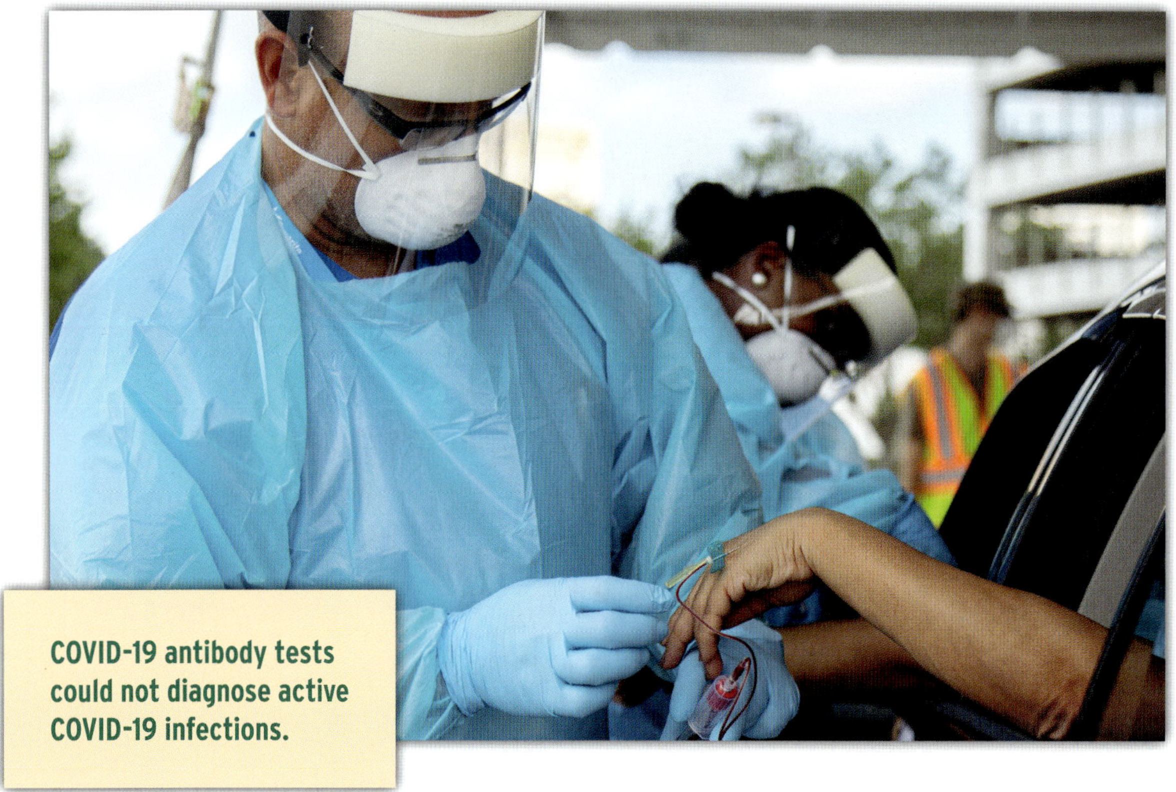

COVID-19 antibody tests could not diagnose active COVID-19 infections.

for the virus's genetic material. Labs could sometimes process these tests in 24 hours. In busy labs, however, processing could take up to a week.

On March 27, the CDC released a rapid COVID-19 test. These tests were administered via nose or throat swab. Instead of looking for genetic material, rapid tests looked for protein fragments on the virus's surface. Rapid tests could return results within 15 minutes. Although quick, the tests were less sensitive than other tests. So, they were more likely to give a negative result to an infected person.

In July, the CDC also developed a COVID-19 antibody test. An antibody test determines whether someone has COVID-19 antibodies. If antibodies are present in the blood, it means a person had and recovered from COVID-19.

Testing procedures varied by state. In some states, patients needed to see a doctor before getting a test. Other states allowed people to be tested without a doctor's visit. Regardless of the state, COVID-19 tests were available for free.

Testing Sites

By summer 2020, the United States no longer faced a testing shortage. So, health officials encouraged people to get tested often. Officials also developed new procedures to make testing safer and more convenient. At-home saliva tests allowed people to take a test at home and mail it to a laboratory. Drive-through testing allowed people to get tested without leaving their cars.

However, some testing sites experienced problems. One drive-through testing site in Phoenix, Arizona, reported a miles-long line on its first day of testing in June. Since drive-through sites were outdoors, medical workers were sometimes exposed to extreme weather. Some sites even had to shut down because of the heat.

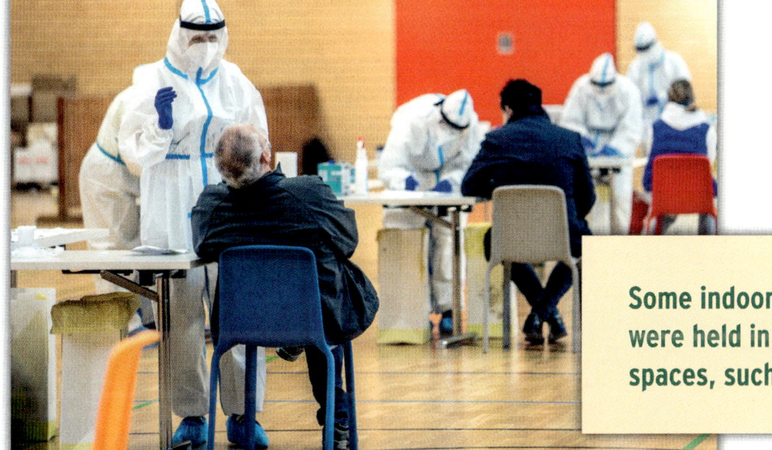

Some indoor COVID-19 test sites were held in large, well-ventilated spaces, such as gymnasiums.

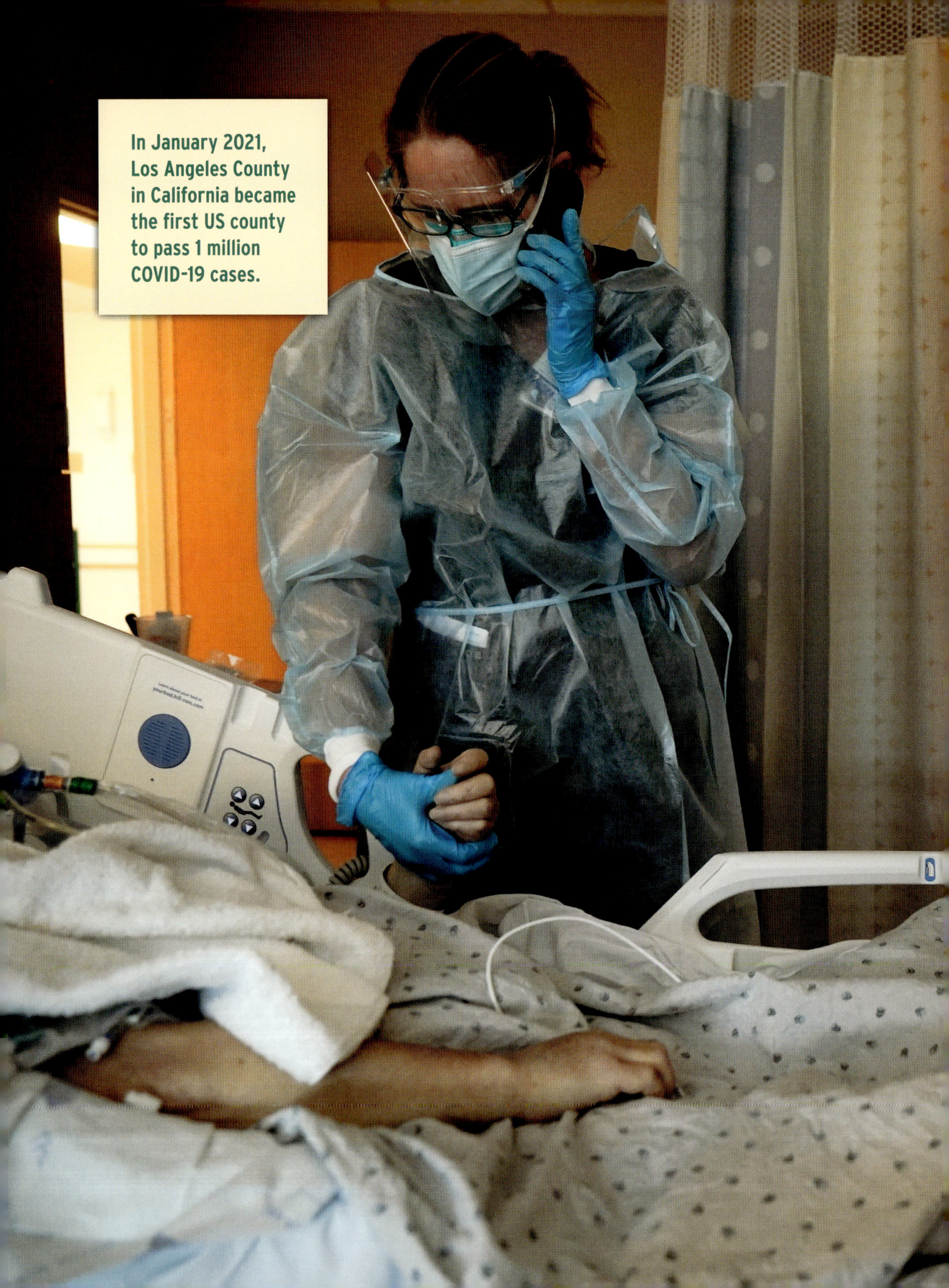

In January 2021,
Los Angeles County
in California became
the first US county
to pass 1 million
COVID-19 cases.

Chapter 6

SPRINTING TOWARD A CURE

As more people were tested, it became clear how widespread COVID-19 had become. In late 2020 and early 2021, the United States regularly recorded more than 200,000 new cases each day. The best hope for beating COVID-19 was developing an effective vaccine. This process typically takes 10 to 15 years. But to stop COVID-19, scientists and drug companies would have to work much faster.

Operation Warp Speed

On March 25, 2020, the US Congress allocated $9.5 billion to vaccine development. This money was given to drug companies around the world whose research looked promising. On May 15, US president Donald Trump announced a new vaccine development program called Operation Warp Speed (OWS). It was committed to delivering 300 million doses of a safe and effective COVID-19 vaccine by 2021. This would be enough to vaccinate nearly the entire US population.

Over the summer, OWS gave additional funds to three drug companies with likely vaccine candidates. The companies were Pfizer, Moderna, and AstraZeneca. If any of the vaccines were authorized for use, the United States was guaranteed a portion of the doses. Other countries that had similarly contributed would also get portions.

By the end of 2020, there were more than 50 COVID-19 vaccines in development. The WHO worked with drug companies and global health leaders to make sure any vaccine would be distributed fairly

Operation Warp Speed was headed by leaders from the CDC, HHS, and other US health organizations.

to countries worldwide. Then doses would be available everywhere and not just in countries able to fund a vaccine's development.

Finding an Antigen

Scientists begin vaccine development by determining which type of antigen is most effective in triggering an immune response. An antigen is usually a small part of a virus or a weakened version of a full virus. But some COVID-19 vaccines took a new approach.

Instead of a virus, the Pfizer and Moderna vaccines contain messenger RNA (mRNA). This is genetic material that tells the body how to make certain proteins. COVID-19 mRNA vaccines instruct the body to create small pieces of the SARS-CoV-2 virus called spike proteins. These proteins are what allow the virus to enter human cells. Spike proteins are harmless on their own. However, the body's immune system still produces antibodies to fight them. These antibodies then attack spike proteins on the real virus if it enters the body, ensuring the virus cannot enter cells and replicate.

The Road to Approval

Once scientists believe they have a promising vaccine, they test it on animals. If the vaccine prevents infection in animals and has no serious side effects, it moves into clinical trials. During clinical trials, researchers test a vaccine on humans.

Clinical trials have three phases. In phase one, a group of healthy adult volunteers takes the vaccine. Researchers study the

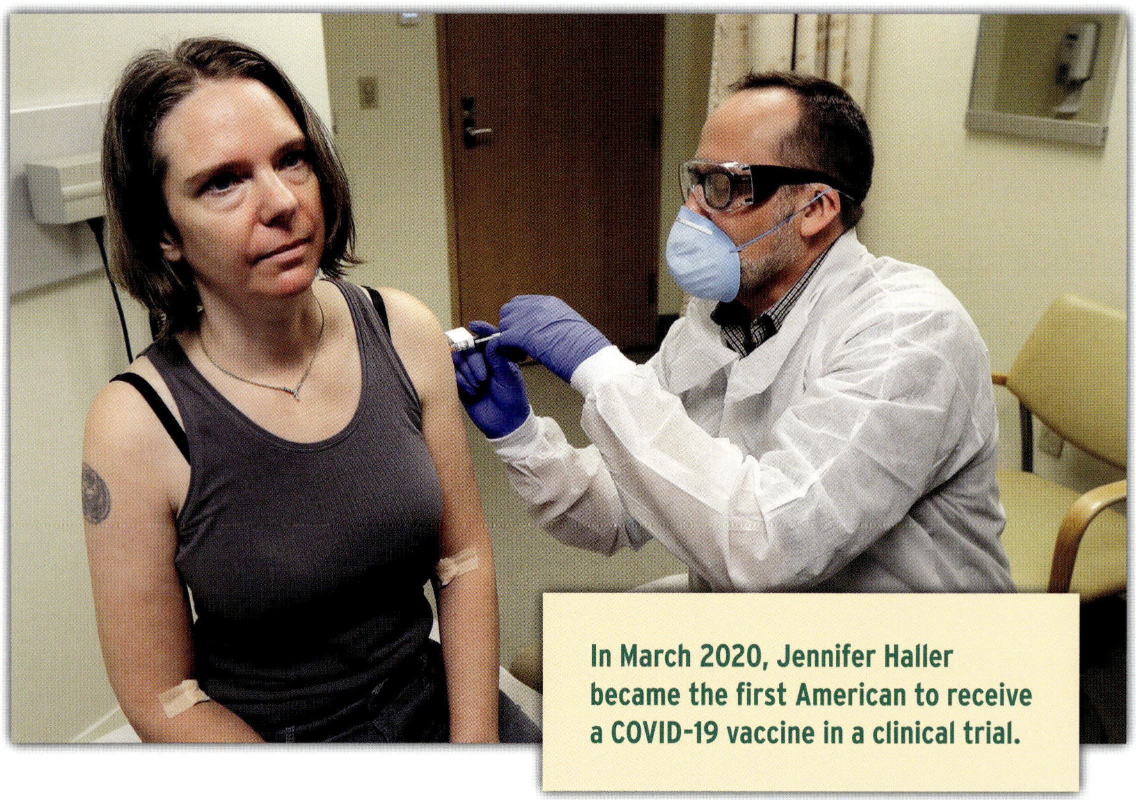

volunteers to see whether their immune systems create antibodies. Researchers also monitor for harmful side effects.

In phase two, a larger, more diverse group of volunteers receives the vaccine. Their reactions are compared to those of a control group of people who didn't receive the vaccine. In phase three, an even larger group of volunteers receives the vaccine. This group is also compared to a control group. In the meantime, researchers monitor volunteers from earlier phases for potential long-term side effects.

Once a vaccine is through clinical trials, it moves to the approval phase. The FDA reviews the data from the trials and determines whether the vaccine is safe for use. Even after a vaccine is approved, researchers continue monitoring it for long-term issues.

Evolving Treatments

A vaccine could not help those who were already severely ill with COVID-19. So, doctors and researchers also tested pharmaceutical treatments for sick patients. On October 22, the FDA said the existing antiviral drug remdesivir could be used to treat COVID-19. On November 19, the FDA also approved the rheumatoid arthritis drug baricitinib combined with remdesivir to treat COVID-19. Studies showed these drugs could help speed a COVID-19 patient's recovery.

The good news kept coming. Several vaccine candidates made it through development and clinical trials in record time. By December, Pfizer, Moderna, and AstraZeneca had all announced success in clinical trials. On December 2, the United Kingdom became the first nation to approve the Pfizer vaccine for use. The FDA authorized Pfizer's vaccine

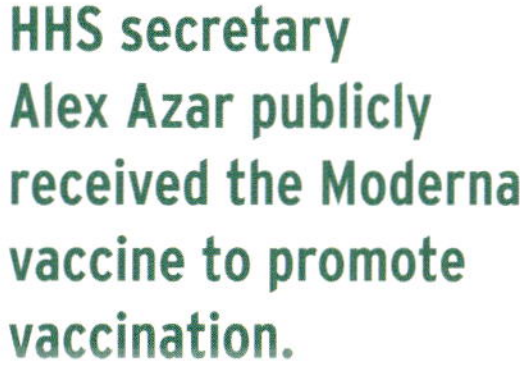

HHS secretary Alex Azar publicly received the Moderna vaccine to promote vaccination.

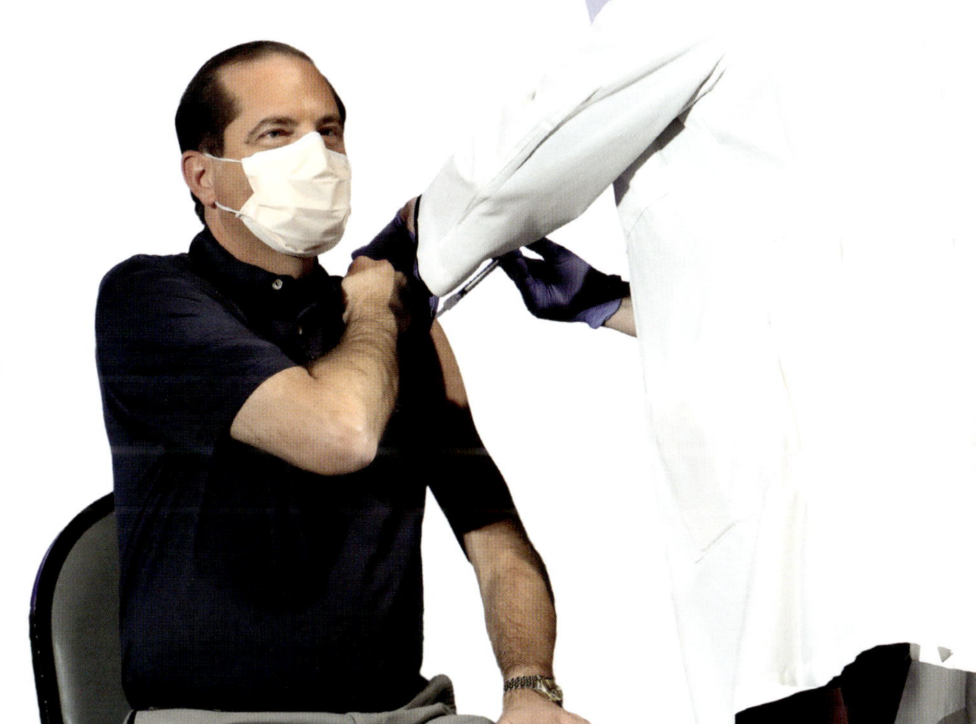

for use in the United States on December 11, and Moderna's vaccine a week later. A vaccine from health-care company Johnson & Johnson was authorized on February 27, 2021.

Distributing the Vaccines

It would take time to manufacture enough vaccines for the entire US population. So, vaccine distribution was first prioritized by need. Frontline health workers were among the first people to be vaccinated. People living in nursing homes or assisted living facilities also received early doses of the vaccines.

Essential workers were next on the list. This group included teachers, transportation workers, and law enforcement officers. In many states, people over the age of 65 were also eligible to receive a vaccine. All vaccines were provided for free at pharmacies and clinics around the country.

The US government believed all adult Americans would be vaccinated by summer 2021. However, some states faced problems vaccinating people quickly. Clinic workers were already overwhelmed helping COVID-19 patients. So, it was sometimes difficult to administer vaccines in a timely manner. Many clinics and pharmacies also faced staffing shortages as workers became sick with COVID-19.

In addition, not everyone was eager to receive a vaccine. Some people believed the vaccines had been approved too quickly and could be dangerous. In December, nearly 40 percent of Americans said they would choose not to get a COVID-19 vaccine. Health officials worked to assure people that the vaccines were safe.

Several COVID-19 vaccines required two shots to be fully effective. By April 2021, more than 97 million Americans had received one dose of a vaccine. Of these, more than 54 million Americans had been fully vaccinated. COVID-19 vaccines gave many people hope that the pandemic would soon be over. In the future, doctors and scientists would use the lessons learned during the COVID-19 pandemic to fight other viruses.

Pharmacists traveled to nursing homes to administer vaccines to residents and workers.

MARCH 1918
The first cases of the 1918 influenza pandemic are reported at Camp Funston in Kansas.

1938
The first influenza vaccine is developed.

1948
The United Nations founds the World Health Organization (WHO).

1919
The 1918 influenza pandemic ends.

1946
The Centers for Disease Control and Prevention (CDC) is founded in Atlanta, Georgia.

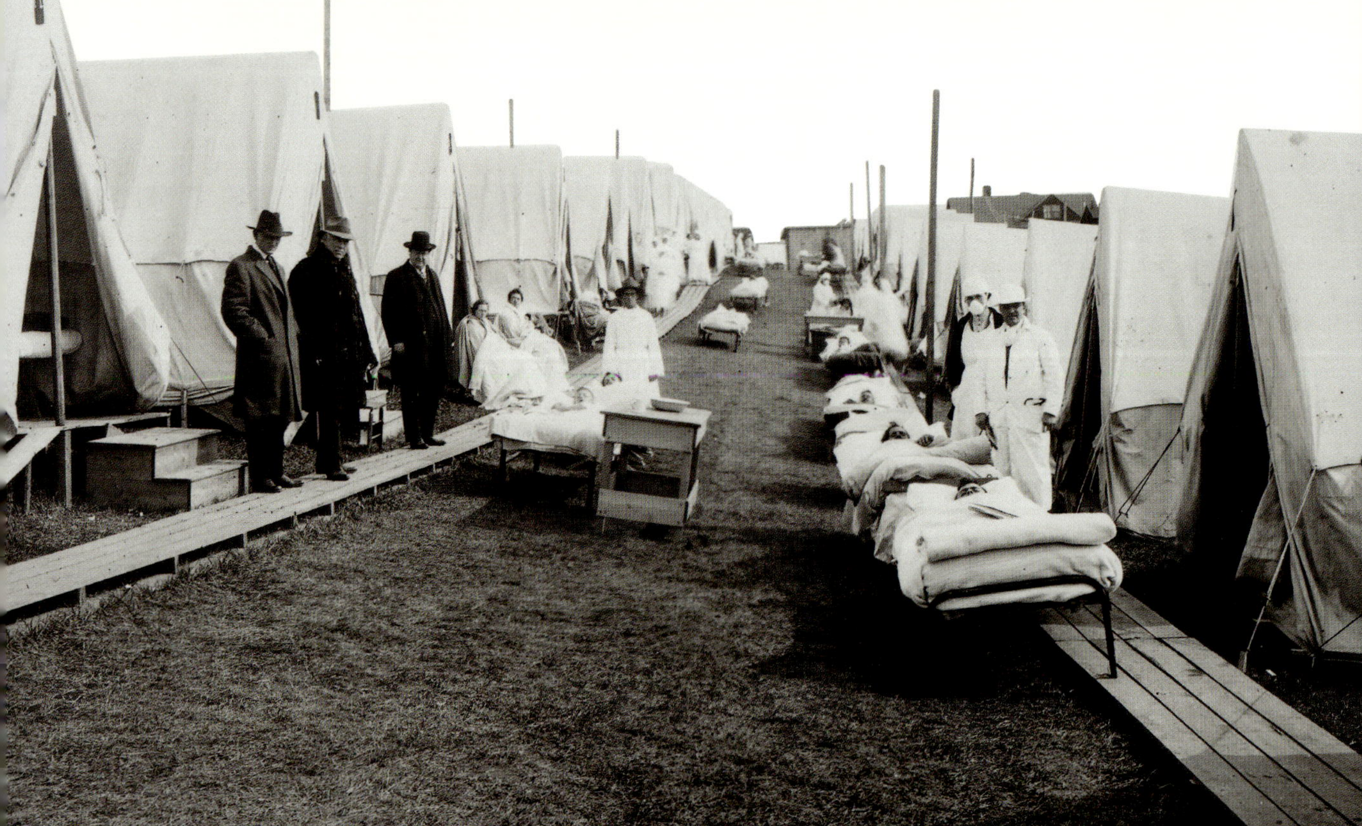

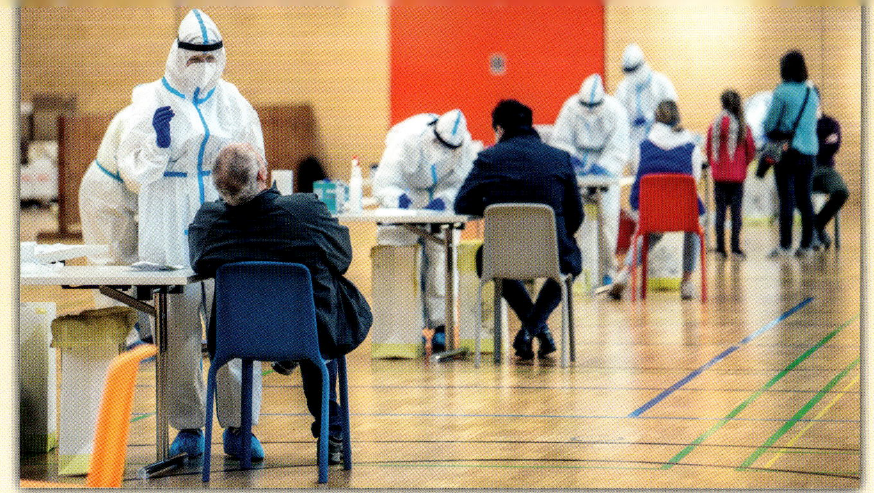

1999

Scientists sequence the full genetic material of the 1918 influenza virus. They use the information to try to understand where the virus came from and what made it deadly.

1977

Scientist Gertrude Elion helps develop acyclovir, the world's first antiviral drug.

DECEMBER 2019

The first cases of COVID-19 are identified in Wuhan, China.

APRIL 2021

More than 97 million Americans have received one dose of a COVID-19 vaccine. Of these, more than 54 million Americans have been fully vaccinated.

MARCH 11, 2020

The WHO declares COVID-19 a pandemic.

OCTOBER 22, 2020

The antiviral drug remdesivir is approved to treat COVID-19.

MAY 15, 2020

US president Donald Trump announces Operation Warp Speed.

DECEMBER 2020

COVID-19 vaccines from drug companies Pfizer and Moderna are authorized for use in the United States.

GLOSSARY

Centers for Disease Control and Prevention (CDC)—the main national health organization in the United States. The CDC works to control the spread of disease and maintain and improve public health in the United States and other countries.

civilian—a person who is not an active member of the military.

diabetes—a disease in which the body cannot properly absorb normal amounts of sugar and starch.

droplet—a tiny drop of liquid.

extract—to withdraw by a physical or chemical process.

genetic—of or relating to a branch of biology that deals with inherited features.

hygiene—conditions or practices of cleanliness that are required for good health.

immune—incapable of being affected by a disease. The immune system protects the body from infection and disease.

infuse—to inject into something.

isolated—separated from others.

microbiologist—a scientist who studies small life-forms.

novel—new and different from what has previously been known.

outbreak—a sudden increase in the occurrence of illness.

overwhelmed—having too much to deal with.

pathologist—a doctor who examines body tissues and fluids that have been affected by disease.

pharmaceutical—of or relating to the manufacture and sale of medical drugs. A pharmacy is a store in which drugs are made and sold.

protocol—a system of rules.

quarantine—to separate from others in order to stop a disease from spreading.

respiratory–having to do with the system of organs involved with breathing.

shortage–a lack of something that is needed.

supplemental–extra or additional.

technician–a person who is skilled at a specific task or method.

United Nations–a group of nations formed in 1945. Its goals are peace, human rights, security, and social and economic development.

ventilated–exposed to fresh, freely moving air.

World Health Organization (WHO)–an agency of the United Nations that works to maintain and improve the health of people around the world.

World War I–from 1914 to 1918, fought in Europe. Great Britain, France, Russia, the United States, and their allies were on one side. Germany, Austria-Hungary, and their allies were on the other side.

ONLINE RESOURCES

To learn more about testing and treatment, please visit **abdobooklinks.com** or scan this QR code. These links are routinely monitored and updated to provide the most current information available.

INDEX